★ IT'S MY STATE! ★
North Carolina

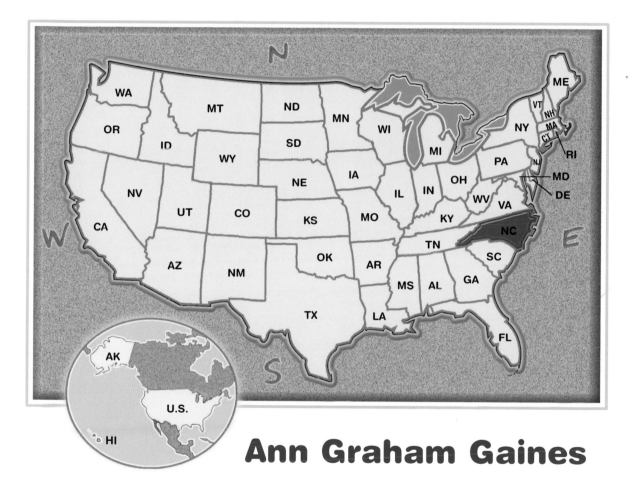

Ann Graham Gaines

MARSHALL CAVENDISH
NEW YORK

Series Consultant

David G. Vanderstel, Ph.D., Executive Director, National Council on Public History

With thanks to Dr. Lynn Getz, Department of History, Appalachian State University, for her expert review of the manuscript.

Benchmark Books
Marshall Cavendish
99 White Plains Road
Tarrytown, New York 10591-9001
www.marshallcavendish.com

Text, maps, and illustrations © 2004 by Marshall Cavendish Corporation
Maps and illustrations by Christopher Santoro

Library of Congress Cataloging-in-Publication Data

Gaines, Ann.
North Carolina / by Ann Graham Gaines;
p. cm. — (It's my state!)
Summary: Surveys the history, geography, government, and economy of
North Carolina as well as the diverse ways of life of its people.
Includes bibliographical references (p.) and index.
ISBN 0-7614-1533-5
1. North Carolina—Juvenile literature. [1. North Carolina.]
I. Title. II. Series.

F254.3 .G35 2003
975.6—dc21
2002156735

Photo research by Candlepants, Inc.

Cover photo:
Back cover illustration: The license plate shows North Carolina's postal abbreviation, followed by its year of statehood.

The photographs in this book are used by permission and through the courtesy of:
Corbis: 33, 36, 73 (middle); Lynda Richardson, 4 (top); Owen Franken, 4 (middle), 49, 54; David Muench, 4 (bottom); Joe McDonald, 5 (middle), 19 (bottom); Raymond Gehman, 5 (bottom); Layne Kennedy, 19 (middle); Buddy Mays, 18 (top); The Mariner's Museum, 26; Bettmann, 27, 38, 39, 40, 41, 43 (bottom), 50 (top), 50 (middle), 51 (top), 51 (bottom); Stapleton Collection, 43 (top); Richard A. Cooke, 46, 73 (top); William A. Bake, 60; Joseph Sohm/ChromoSohm, Inc., 72 (top); Tom Nebbia, 72 (middle); Charles O'Rear, 72 (bottom). *AnimalsAnimals / Earth Scenes:* David M. Dennis, 19 (top). *PhotoResearchers, Inc.:* Jack Dermid, 5 (top); Michael P. Gadomski, 18 (middle). *Getty Images:* Ron Chapple, 44. *Index Stock Imagery:* Ron Mellott, 17; John Greim, 18 (bottom); Larry Lipsky, 20; Jon Riley, 47; Wendell Metzen, 57; Mark Segal, 65; Steve Dunwell, 74. *Envision:* Andre Baranowski, 68; Zeva Oelbaum, 73 (bottom). *Bridgeman Art Library:* Library of Congress, Washington D.C., 30. *Gibson Stock Photography:* 66. *RobertStock.com:* G. Ahrens, 13; H. Abernathy, 15; R. Krubner, 53; R. Gilbert, 63. *Transparencies, Inc.:* 10, 11, 12, 21, 55, 56, 58, 59, 69, 71. *Simpson's Nature Photography:* 14. *AirPhoto / Jim Wark:* 8. *Photograph by Paul Buchanan:* 22. *Art Resource, NY:* New York Public Library, 24, 32; National Portrait Gallery, Smithsonian Institution, 50 (bottom), 51 (middle).

Series design by Anahid Hamparian
Printed in Italy

1 3 5 6 4 2

Contents

A Quick Look at North Carolina

Nickname: Tar Heel State or Old North State
Population: 8,049,313 (2000)
Statehood: 1789

Bird: Cardinal

The North Carolina legislature chose the cardinal as the state bird in 1943. Cardinals live in North Carolina year-round in huge numbers. Also known as the winter redbird, this fine singer can be spotted across the state.

Flower: Flowering Dogwood

The dogwood is actually a flowering tree. Dogwoods grow all over the state—from the mountains to the coast. They begin to flower in the spring, but new blooms continue to appear through the summer.

Tree: Longleaf Pine

The longleaf pine is the state's official tree. In the colonial era, these trees were used for resin, turpentine, and timber. All of these materials were needed for ships. Today lumber companies and farmers still grow pine, for use in buildings and furniture.

Dog: Plott Hound

This hunting dog was first bred in the mountains of North Carolina around 1750. The hounds were used to hunt wild boars. These gentle and loyal dogs are also skilled trackers. The Plott Hound is one of only four breeds of dog known to have started in the United States.

Reptile: Eastern Box Turtle

Eastern box turtles live throughout eastern North Carolina. They can be found living in forests or fields. Box turtles eat plants, worms, insects, mushrooms, and snails. The legislature chose them as a state symbol because they are a "model of patience for mankind, and [remind us] . . . of our State's unrelenting pursuit of great and lofty goals."

Rock: Granite

Beautiful North Carolina granite has been used in buildings and monuments all over the United States. The world's largest open-faced granite quarry is located in Surry County. The quarry is 1 mile long.

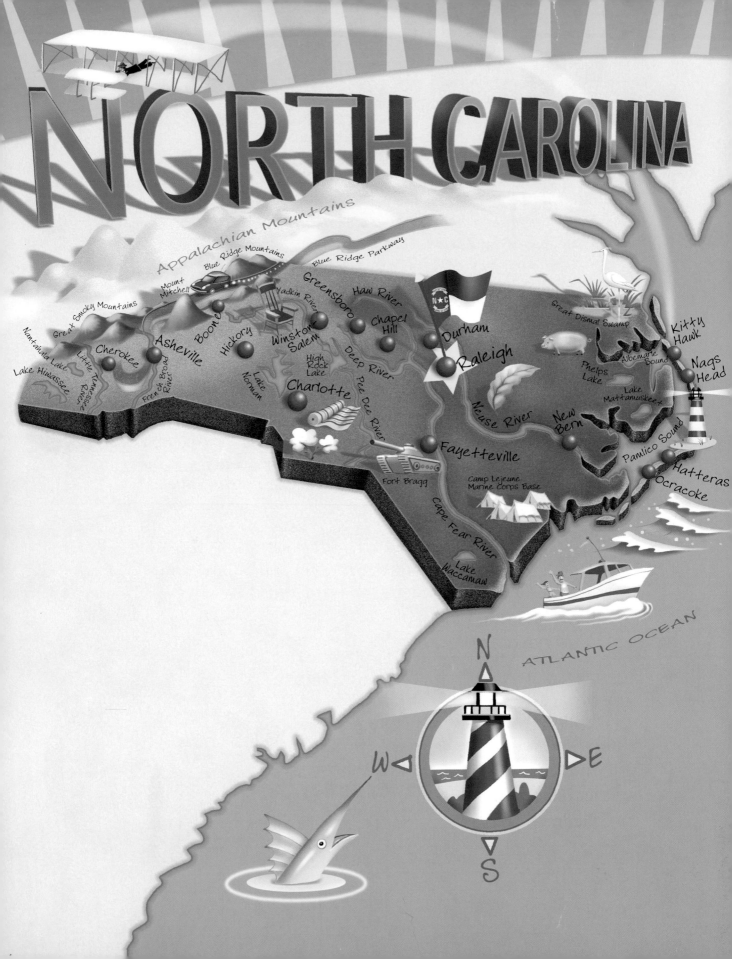

1 The Tar Heel State

North Carolina measures about 500 miles from east to west and 150 miles from north to south. The state can easily be crossed by car in less than a day. This means that the people who live in the larger cities in the state's center can easily reach the state's beautiful beaches, lush forests, and rugged mountains.

North Carolina is bounded on one side by the Appalachian Mountains and by the Atlantic Ocean on the other. The state's northern boundary, which it shares with Virginia, is almost straight. Its southern border, which separates North Carolina from South Carolina and Georgia, looks very bumpy on a map.

With its wide variety of landscapes, North Carolina is a state known for its great beauty. To the east lie the shore and the islands of the Outer Banks. The coastal plain, a flat and often marshy area, is found a little farther inland. In the center of the state, in the broad region called the Piedmont, gently rolling hills are crisscrossed by small rivers and streams. Centuries ago, forests covered the Piedmont.

North Carolina's Borders

North: Virginia
East: The Atlantic Ocean
South: South Carolina and Georgia
West: Tennessee

Today, there are fewer trees, but groves still fill the region, even in the area's many cities. To the west, North Carolina grows rugged and more wild. Mountain chains stand tall on the horizon. All of these add to the list of natural wonders found in the Tar Heel State.

The Outer Banks

North Carolina land does not end at the mainland's shore. The Outer Banks islands sit just off of the state's coast. These islands are long and narrow and formed mostly of sand. They protect North Carolina's mainland from the blasts of waves and occasional storms. When hurricanes hit, the islands absorb much of their force and suffer more damage than inland areas. Channels of water run between these islands. The channels are filled with reefs and shifting sand bars. Over the centuries the channels have been the sites of shipwrecks. The area is given the name "The Graveyard of the Atlantic" since more than six hundred shipwrecks have occurred there since the sixteenth century.

This aerial view shows some of the islands of the Outer Banks.

In the days before European settlers came to North Carolina, Native Americans known as the Hatteras camped on the Outer Banks islands every summer. They went there to fish, gather clams, catch turtles, and hunt waterfowl. When the English settlers arrived in the 1580s, they built their earliest settlement on one of the islands. The settlement was called Roanoke, and the island still bears that name today. Unfortunately, the settlement failed. For many years afterward, few people made the Outer Banks their home. When brave souls did establish villages there, they faced a life of isolation.

During the 1700s, the Outer Banks were often used by pirates. The islands and coves were ideal for hiding their ships and treasures.

Until about fifty years ago, the islands could be reached only by boat. Despite the fact that the islands are a nice vacation spot, few tourists made the trip there. In the 1950s the state built a bridge and connected the islands to the mainland. Tourists began to flock to the Outer Banks using this highway.

Around the same time, the U.S. government bought a great deal of land on the islands and created two national seashores. The islands also have nature preserves where wildlife is protected. On the preserves roads are built only where they will not disturb the wildlife. Outside the preserves, however, private landowners have recently built many hotels, condominiums, and shopping malls.

Today many visit the islands during the warm summer months. They come to enjoy the beach, play in the water, collect shells, and to fish. Bird-watchers visit year-round to see the different seabirds. These include many varieties of gull, long-legged herons, egrets, and osprey.

Outer Banks beaches are popular spots on hot days.

Although the booming tourist industry helps the state's economy it also creates serious problems. People concerned for the environment worry about how humans affect the islands' ecosystems. They point out that too many visitors harm plants and animals. Scientists noticed that since the Outer Banks have undergone many changes—such as construction of buildings and other structures—the islands no longer protect the mainland coast as well as before.

The Coast and the Plain Beyond

Several broad shallow sounds, or bays, separate the Outer Banks and North Carolina's mainland. Here the long curving shoreline dips in and out. This gives North Carolina the longest inland shoreline in the United States. In some places, waves lapping onshore have formed tiny harbors. In other places, rivers—which often flow slowly as they near the ocean—have formed deltas. These are places where a river breaks into many smaller channels. People take advantage of these small waterways and raise seafood in them.

Along the shore, the land is often wet and swampy. Waterbirds and some alligators make their homes there. Over the years, towns have appeared along the coast. In the past, mostly fishers lived in them. But today more and more retired people have moved to the area, drawn by its quiet and restful pace.

A little farther inland, the coastal plain begins. Its land is low and level. There are many swamps and shallow lakes in this region and the soil usually stays moist. In some places grasslands have appeared. The soil in parts of the plain is good for growing tobacco, peanuts, soybeans, and sweet potatoes. Early landowners built North Carolina's first plantations in the low country around Cape Fear in the early eighteenth century. Many of these plantations grew rice. Eventually, a number of towns and small farms were established.

The city of Wilmington is on the coastal plain. Located near the mouth of the Cape Fear River, this city is the state's most important port.

The Great Dismal Swamp, located in the eastern and very northern part of the state, is one of the unique features of the coastal plain. This huge wetland also crosses into Virginia. For years, few people lived there because it was hard to build roads or towns. Canals had to be dug first before people could set up communities.

Cypress, moss, and other plants grow in the wet environment of the Great Dismal Swamp.

The Piedmont

A fall line—a place where the elevation suddenly rises—separates the coastal plain from the wide region known as the Piedmont. Along the fall line's eastern edge, the elevation stays fairly low, ranging from 300 to 600 feet above sea level. But moving west across the Piedmont, the land rises, reaching as high as 1,500 feet above sea level at the foot of the Blue Ridge Mountains. Hills with round tops and long, low ridges are spread across the Piedmont. The area also has some low mountains, such as the Uwharrie. Small rivers and streams cut across the region inviting residents and visitors alike to raft, canoe, and fish on them.

Much of the Piedmont has red soil that is rich in clay. This often makes it hard to grow a wide range of crops. But one crop that does thrive in the region is tobacco. For centuries farmers made a living of tobacco farming. Today some farmers still do.

At one time, many decades ago, the Piedmont was a thriving farming region. In recent times, the area has changed. All of the state's biggest cities, including Charlotte, Winston-Salem, Greensboro, Raleigh, and Durham, are located in the Piedmont. While part of the population still makes its living from the land, most residents live and work in these large cities. Many have jobs in schools, universities, stores, offices, and factories.

The plowed land of this farm shows the red clay soil of the Piedmont.

The Mountains

Beyond the Piedmont lies North Carolina's mountain region. It includes many different ranges, all of which form part of the huge Appalachian mountain chain. Several Appalachian peaks have been worn down by wind, rain, and snow. As a result, these peaks are no longer rough and jagged. Some appear rounded or even flat at the top. Steep valleys and gorges plunge between the peaks. Some of the valleys are laced with sparkling waterfalls.

The Blue Ridge Mountains rise sharply from the western edge of the Piedmont, running northeast to southwest. The government has built a scenic highway—a road designed to provide great views—through the mountains. The National Park Service takes care of the Blue Ridge Parkway and the many tourists that travel it every year. The region's main city, Asheville, lies near the parkway.

A drive along the Blue Ridge Parkway offers views of North Carolina's striking landscape.

Beyond the Blue Ridge Mountains lies a broad, high plateau. A plateau is a portion of flat land that is raised above the surrounding land. Beyond that plateau, the Blue Ridge Mountains run parallel to the Great Smoky Mountains. Early English explorers named both of these ranges after the smoky blue haze that often covers their peaks. A large part of the Smokies has been made into a national park.

A blue haze hangs over the Great Smoky Mountains.

Other, smaller ranges also make an appearance in the region, stretching from east to west. These include the Bald, Black, Brush, Iron, South, Stone, and Unaka Mountains. The Black Mountains contain the state's highest peak, Mount Mitchell, which rises 6,684 feet above sea level. It is the highest peak in the United States east of the Mississippi River. The peak is a part of Mount Mitchell State Park. Founded in 1915, it was North Carolina's first state park.

In the nineteenth century, mining became an important industry in the mountains. In many mountain valleys there is still rich, fertile land that is good for farming. In the past some of the region's forests were cleared for lumber and to make room for people's farms and homes. But many dense forests remain. In the autumn, sightseers pile into their cars to drive through the mountains to see the trees' spectacular colors as the leaves turn red, gold, orange, and yellow.

North Carolina's Waters

There are no major waterways in the state but many rivers, streams, and lakes can be found across North Carolina. Some of North Carolina's rivers are deep enough for big boats to travel. Some people with smaller boats, however, spend time on the narrower, faster-flowing rivers. For example, the Nantahala River is ideal for white water rafting. Its name,

Some of North Carolina's state parks have stunning waterfalls.

which means the "land of the noonday sun," reflects the fact that sunlight reaches the floor of its gorge only for a short time each afternoon. The state's largest natural lake, Lake Mattamuskeet, is a popular spot in the warm months.

Weather

North Carolina has a mild climate. Springtime in the state is wet and warm, but the summers can be hot. In the Piedmont, the humidity, or moisture in the air, can be very high. In the days before air conditioning, some families living in the Piedmont would close up their houses and spend every July at the shore or at mountain resorts. On many summer days in the southern part of the state, the temperature can rise to more than 80 degrees Fahrenheit. In general, it is cooler on the eastern coast and in the mountains to the west.

The state's location on the Atlantic coast often makes it a target for tropical storms and hurricanes. These severe storms cause floods and destroy many homes and buildings.

In the fall, the temperatures are milder. With the cooler temperatures, the leaves on many trees begin to change color. The North Carolina hills and forests become beautiful seas of red, orange, and yellow. As winter draws closer, the temperatures begin to fall even further. Winters in the mountains are more severe than in other parts of the state. The mountain regions usually get enough snow to draw skiers and snowboarders. In the Piedmont and on the coastal plain, there are many winter days when the temperature falls below freezing. Snow does fall, and sometimes blizzards hit, but in general, these regions receive little snow.

The state gets a lot of rain. The most rain falls in the mountains and along the Atlantic coast.

Wildlife

The variety of land features and the moderate weather make the state an ideal home for a wide range of plants. Many different types of grasses grow along the fields and hills. About two-thirds of North Carolina is covered in forests. The trees that make up these forests include different types of ash, birch, cedar, pine, elm, and maple. Trees such as tupelo and cypress dot the swamps and wetlands. The mountainous regions are filled with fir, spruce, and oak. Across the state you might find wildflowers such as blood root, lilies, trillium, azaleas, and various rhododendron.

In the fall the state's many trees turn brilliant shades of orange, red, and yellow.

Plants & Animals

Red Maple

The red maple is a large tree that grows wild in the mountains of North Carolina. People across the state also plant them in their yards. In the fall, the leaves of these maples turn brilliant colors. The fruit of the red maple looks like a small pair of papery wings.

Serviceberry

The serviceberry is a tree that grows in the mountains of North Carolina. It can grow to be anywhere from 2 to 50 feet tall. In the spring, the tree has clusters of white flowers. By summertime, the tree is covered with dark red berries. Many birds, raccoons, mice, and squirrels like to eat these berries.

Feral Horse

For hundreds of years feral horses roamed free on the islands of North Carolina. Scientists believe that these horses may be related to the horses brought to the region by Spanish explorers who came to the area hundreds of years ago. Today many feral horses live in specific, protected areas, where they feed on marsh grasses and other plants. A small group of feral horses lives on Ocracoke Island in the Outer Banks.

Venus's-flytrap

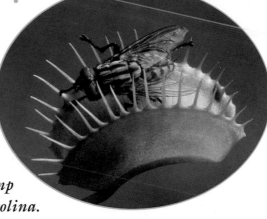

Venus's-flytrap is a plant that catches and digests insects. The plant has bright green leaves that are hinged like a trap. The leaves are ringed with spikes or bristles. When an insect brushes against these bristles, the leaf snaps shut. The leaf stays closed until the insect has been digested. Venus's-flytraps can be found in the damp coastal regions of North and South Carolina.

Red Wolf

In the past, many red wolves were hunted and killed. Their natural habitats have been destroyed by land developments. As a result, red wolves are an endangered species. The U.S. government has started a program to try to return the red wolf to the northeastern corner of the state. Because of these efforts and the increased awareness of the wolves' situation, the red wolf population is slowly growing.

Southern Flying Squirrel

Extra folds of skin stretched between the front and hind legs help this small mammal to glide from branch to branch. The tail, which is long and flattened, is used to help control the squirrel's glide. This squirrel can be brown or gray, has large dark eyes, and usually comes out at night.

North Carolina has an assortment of mammals, reptiles, fish, and amphibians. Wild animals roam through the forests and mountain chains. The bear population is small, but there are many deer. Foxes, squirrels, opossums, raccoons, skunks, and rabbits make their homes in the state's woods and fields. Beaver and otter swim in the rivers.

Every autumn, groups of monarch butterflies from northern regions fly south for the winter. They stop in North Carolina before they continue their journey to Mexico.

As for birds, scientists say that North Carolina is great for bird watching. Many different species live in North Carolina. Birdwatchers gather to see small birds such as whip-poor-wills, hooded warblers, and gnatcatchers. Larger birds, such as ducks, geese, and swans, spend the winter along the coast. Wild turkeys roam across North Carolina.

The waters are also filled with wildlife. Frogs, newts, and other amphibians live in or near the water. Freshwater fish such as trout, bass, and sunfish are found in the state's rivers, streams, and lakes. In the coastal waters, you might see dolphins, marlin, sailfish, and sturgeon.

Small populations of eastern cougar live in North Carolina. These large cats feed on deer and small mammals.

Some animals, such as the eastern puma, the leatherback sea turtle, and the spruce-fir moss spider are endangered. This means that their populations are very small. Scientists and concerned residents work hard to protect the remaining populations. Laws are passed to prevent people from harming these animals and their habitats. Breeding programs also help the endangered animals. Additionally, North Carolina has nature preserves and national wildlife refuges designed to protect the state's plants and animals. In these areas, the wildlife is able to multiply and survive. Humans are not allowed to develop the land. But many often go to see the animals and plants in their natural habitat.

Six species—or types—of fish are found only in North Carolina. These are the Waccamaw darter, Waccamaw killifish, Waccamaw silverside, Cape Fear shiner, Pinewoods shiner, and the Carolina madtorn.

A hike through Mitchell State Park gives this family an opportunity to experience and learn about North Carolina's wildlife.

2 From the Beginning

North America's earliest inhabitants were most likely the ancestors of today's Native Americans. These early people came from Asia using a land bridge that joined Siberia to Alaska. It is also possible that they traveled across the Pacific Ocean and arrived in boats. Later generations kept moving south, deeper into the continent. More than 10,000 years ago, Native Americans settled in what is now North Carolina.

Native Americans

The Native Americans thrived in this region. The land was rich in natural resources. There were many animals in the forests and the waterways were filled with fish. Some natives permanently settled in the area. Others traveled around but returned once a year.

When European settlers arrived in the late sixteenth century, there were three main groups of Native Americans living there. The Algonquian lived along the coast. They fished in the inlets near their settlements. These inlets—small inland bodies of water

These boys were part of a family living in North Carolina's mountains in the 1920s and 1930s.

A colored engraving shows what an Algonquian village may have looked like in the sixteenth century.

that lead to larger bodies of water—were salty because they were connected to the Atlantic Ocean. The Algonquian also hunted in freshwater swamps. At one time, as many as 5,000 Algonquian lived on Hatteras Island. Around 1584, 7,000 Algonquian lived on the islands and coast of what is now North Carolina. However, their numbers quickly declined once European settlers moved into the region. Many natives died from famine when their hunting and fishing grounds were taken over. Diseases brought by the settlers further reduced the Algonquian population. By the 1770s, all of the Carolina Algonquian had died from famine or disease.

The Catawba were a group of different tribes. All of these tribes spoke the same Siouan language. Not much is known about the culture and traditions of the Catawba who lived in the area during the late sixteenth century. One reason might be that the Catawba and early settlers did not interact often. It is known, however, that the Catawba lived in the forested hills of the Piedmont. There were about 6,000 living in the region when Europeans arrived.

The Cherokee lived farther inland in the hardwood forests of the Blue Ridge and Great Smoky Mountains. They were the last of the North Carolinian Indians to come into contact with Europeans. They farmed and hunted, utilizing the land and its resources. Cherokee communities were often surrounded by tall wooden fences called palisades. Early Cherokee homes were probably carved out of the hillsides, with log walls and a roof made of bark. Eventually, the Cherokee began to make their homes out of clay and wood. However, as more settlers came to the region, the Cherokee lost their land and were forced to either move or learn the settlers' ways and culture.

European Exploration

An explorer named Giovanni da Verrazzano was the first European believed to reach the coast of North Carolina. The king of France had sent him in search of the Northwest Passage. Europeans believed that this trade route would lead them through North America and into Asia. Verrazzano passed Cape Fear in 1524. He thought the Outer Banks islands actually formed an isthmus, which is a long finger of land stretching out into the sea. In a report to the king, he said that the stretch of ocean beyond this land must be the Oriental sea.

Verrazzano believed that the "faire fields and plains" he saw and the friendly native peoples he met meant that this new land would be a good place to live. But France did not send any settlers there to test the explorer's suggestion. Two years later, Spain established a settlement near Cape Fear. It was the first European country to establish a settlement in the region. The Spanish colony quickly came to a sad end, however, when many of its residents starved or died of illness.

In 1540, conquistador Hernando de Soto became the next Spaniard to come to the area. While exploring, he and his large party of soldiers traveled through the land that is now Florida, along the Mississippi River, and beyond. They crossed the southwestern tip of North Carolina's mountains. They did not establish settlements, and De Soto died along the way. Some of his men eventually returned to Spain and reported that they never found the gold they were looking for. Still, in the thirty years that followed, other Spanish explorers continued to travel north from Florida. The Spanish government was not interested in settling new lands, so no more Spaniards were sent to establish colonies in North Carolina.

England, on the other hand, became greatly interested in settling the area. In 1584, two English ships reached the Outer Banks, searching for a place to anchor their ships. The vessels' captains were sent there by Sir Walter Raleigh. Raleigh was a government official who wanted to help the queen expand the English empire as well as learn more about the North American coast. When the explorers returned to England with news that they had found an ideal place, he decided to colonize the area.

Raleigh himself never came to the region, but he paid others to move to present-day North Carolina. They founded a colony on Roanoke Island in 1585.

This map shows English settlers arriving near Roanoke.

North Carolina

The Lost Colony

The island colony of Roanoke was not successful. In less than a year, the first settlers decided that life on the island was too hard and returned to England. Sir Walter Raleigh persuaded new recruits to go to the island in 1587. This time John White led the group. He was a wealthy Englishman who was interested in studying the island's plant and animal life. One hundred ten settlers, including seventeen women and nine children, arrived on Roanoke Island in July. They repaired the cottages that had been built by the earlier settlers and rebuilt an abandoned fort on the northern end of the island. Less than a month after they arrived, White's daughter gave birth to a baby girl. Virginia Dare was the first English child born on American soil.

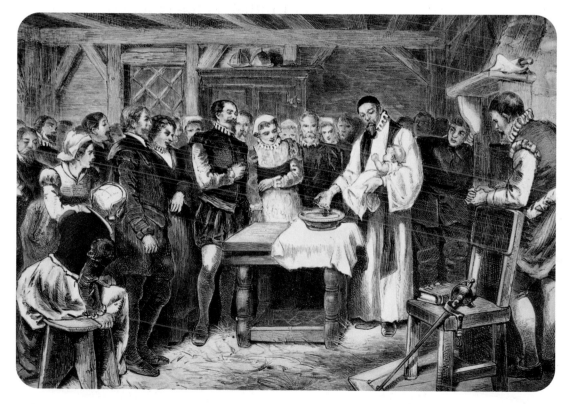

The colonists at Roanoke look on as Virginia Dare is baptized.

Soon the colonists realized that they needed more supplies. White took a ship and sailed back to England for food, tools, and more settlers. Before leaving Roanoke, he and the settlers agreed that if they decided to move their growing town, they would carve a message onto a tree, saying where they had gone.

White did not return to Roanoke Island until 1590. When he did, he found the settlement and the fort in ruins. All the colonists had vanished. Two messages were carved into trees, as the settlers had agreed. CRO was scratched onto one tree trunk and CROATOAN on another. White thought that the settlers had gone south to live with the friendly Croatan Indians on Hatteras Island. But when he went there, he did not find the settlers. He eventually gave up his search and returned to England. Raleigh sent other parties in search of the missing settlers, but they were never found.

The fate of the Lost Colony of Roanoke has long been one of America's great historical mysteries. One possible answer recently emerged. In 1993, archaeologists digging in Buxton, North Carolina, found artifacts from an old Croatan community. They think that it is possible that some of the items that they found, such as lead bullets, broken pottery, and copper coins, belonged to the Roanoke settlers. Perhaps they lived, at least for a time, with their Croatan neighbors.

Successful Settlement

Despite the failure of the Roanoke colony, England pushed ahead with its plans to settle the land that includes present-day North Carolina. The king considered it part of his Virginia colony. In 1629, King Charles I granted the area that includes North and South Carolina to a lord named Robert Heath. By

1650, English settlers had moved into the northeastern corner of North Carolina. They had come from Virginia looking for fertile land on which to grow crops such as tobacco. At the time, tobacco was so valuable that the crops could be sold for close to their weight in gold.

The settlers liked North Carolina and prospered there. Soon word spread about the benefits of life in this rich and beautiful land and more settlers arrived. In 1663, King Charles II transferred the rights to Heath's grant to eight other men. These proprietors, as they were called, named their new lands Carolina in his honor ("Carolus" means Charles in Latin). In 1710, the proprietors of Carolina divided it into two separate colonies, called quite simply North Carolina and South Carolina. Each of the new colonies had its own governor.

As the Carolinas prospered, problems arose for the area's native residents. Many Native Americans had died when the Europeans first came. Many died from smallpox—a disease their bodies could not fight. The growing number of settlers now wanted more and more land. They expected the Native Americans to move away from the coast, making more room for settlements. In 1711, the Tuscarora decided to try and scare the settlers into leaving the area. They killed more than one hundred settlers. The English fought back in 1713, killing and capturing hundreds of tribe members. This ended the Tuscarora rebellion, which was one of the last real efforts made by eastern Native Americans to make Europeans abandon their colonies. After it was over, settlers moved into more of North Carolina. By 1720, there were 36,000 people of European descent living in North Carolina.

In 1729, North Carolina's proprietors sold the colony back to the king of England. From then on, the king chose the governors who ran the colony. He also called for the formation of a legislature to help govern the colony. All the while, North Carolina continued to grow and prosper. Its plantations, worked by slaves, grew not only tobacco, but other valuable crops as well. Visitors wrote that its cities had fine houses and well-stocked stores. One thing the colony did lack was a permanent seat of government. The legislature met in different places. Sometimes it assembled in a delegate's home. At other times, it met in a town courthouse. Finally in 1766, New Bern, located in the eastern part of the colony, was chosen as the colony's capital. A governor's mansion was built there in 1771. The colony continued to expand and

Governor Tryon, shown speaking to angry colonists, chose New Bern as North Carolina's first colonial capital.

many settlers began to cross the mountains and move into the western parts of North Carolina. They also started to settle in the region that includes parts of present-day Kentucky and Tennesee.

Revolution

In the 1770s, more colonists in North Carolina, as in the other colonies, grew unhappy with British rule. The colonists felt that they were taxed too heavily, and were angry that they could not represent themselves in the British parliament that met in London. Some became deeply committed to the cause of independence. Colonists wanted to hurt Britain's economy by refusing to buy British goods.

A plaque in North Carolina's state capital honors a group of fifty-one women who gathered at a tea party in Edenton in 1774. They decided that they would all stop buying both British tea and clothing. This event is the "earliest known instance of political activity on the part of women in the American colonies."

One of North Carolina's most important acts of resistance to British rule was the Halifax Resolves. This was a protest document that expressed North Carolina's anger with the British government. In 1776, every colony sent delegates to the Second Continental Congress, where they discussed independence. On April 12, 1776, North Carolina became the first colony to vote in favor of breaking from British rule.

The American Revolution was a difficult time for the people of North Carolina. Many men and boys joined the Revolutionary Army and fought in the war. Some battles were fought on North Carolina soil. The biggest battle occurred at the town called Guilford Courthouse in 1781. During the war, North Carolinians also protected their homes and did what they could to support the

Nearly 4,000 American troops fought British soldiers at the Battle of Guilford Courthouse.

colonial troops. British general Cornwallis became so angry when the people of Charlotte refused to cooperate with him that he called the place a "hornet's nest." The people of Charlotte were so proud of this that they eventually added the words to their city seal.

The Revolutionary War officially ended in 1783. The former colonies, now called states, all belonged to a single union. The Constitution was written, and the new nation was called the United States. North Carolina officially became a state in 1789.

During the 1780s, North Carolina was much larger than it is today. Its lands stretched west all the way to the Mississippi River. In 1789, the state gave its far western lands to the U.S. government. These lands eventually became part of Tennessee, which officially became a state in 1796.

The people of North Carolina decided it was time to build a new capital city. Officials chose Wake County, in the center of the state, as its location and bought 1,000 acres of land there.

They decided to name the new capital city Raleigh, after the sponsor of the Roanoke colony.

The 1800s

In the early nineteenth century, the state of North Carolina continued to grow and prosper. The state already had a fine university, the University of North Carolina, which was the nation's first public university to open its doors to students. Soon more colleges and universities were founded in the state. Raleigh became a city of culture, where people enjoyed art, music, and the theater. Other cities thrived in the Piedmont region.

Farms had long been an important part of the state's economy. By the 1860s there were more than 50,000 farms in North Carolina. The state also had hundreds of small plantations. Many of these farms and plantations grew crops such as tobacco and cotton. Slaves were needed to work the fields. As a result, slavery helped to make North Carolina's economy strong. Some people, called abolitionists, were against slavery. However, most North Carolinans believed that slavery was a necessary part of the economy. They did not want slavery to be abolished, or ended. There were political debates about slavery in North Carolina and around the country.

African-American farmworkers are holding bushels of cotton in the fields where they work.

Making a Homemade Doll

An attic in a very old North Carolina house held a small historical treasure—a simple handmade doll. This toy probably belonged to the child of a slave who lived in the house more than one hundred years ago. Most slaves did not have many possessions, but parents sometimes made toys for their children using household items. You can make a similar doll by following these instructions.

What You Need

Piece of paper at least 8 1/2 by 11 inches
Pencil with eraser
Scissors
Ballpoint pen
Sewing pins
Two pieces of felt, at least 8 1/2 by 11 inches
Stapler—smaller staples are recommended
18 square inches of polyester or cotton batting cut into pieces, or two or three
   pairs of old pantyhose
One piece of narrow ribbon, about 2 feet long

With the pencil, draw the outline of the doll's body on the paper. Be sure to make the doll large enough so that you will not have problems cutting and putting it together. The bottom of the body should line up with the bottom of the paper.

Draw a second line 1/2 inch outside your outline, all the way around the doll's

body. Cut along this outside line. Stack both pieces of felt and pin the paper on the top. Trace the outline onto the felt using the ballpoint pen. Unpin the paper.

Pin the two pieces of felt together. Cut around your tracing. Staple near the edge of the felt. Staple all the edges except at the bottom. Stuff the doll with the batting or pantyhose. Staple the bottom closed.

Draw a face on the doll with the ballpoint pen and tie the ribbon around its neck. You can show your doll to your family and friends, pretending that you have found a historic artifact from the past.

Tensions were rising between the northern and southern states. Most northern states did not have agricultural economies like the southern states. As a result, they did not need slaves and opposed slavery. Besides disagreeing with the North's stand on slavery, many of the southern states were unhappy with the federal government. They felt that the states were not given enough rights and that the national government had too much control. These issues led to the Civil War.

The nation was divided between northern states that still belonged to the Union, and southern states that formed the Confederacy. In 1861, North Carolina was the last of the southern states to secede, or separate, from the Union. During the war, North Carolina supplied more men to the Confederate Army than any other state. North Carolina also lost more soldiers than any other Confederate state.

Many important Civil War events occurred in North Carolina. Battles such as the bloody Battle of Bentonville, took

On March 19, 1865, Union troops defeated Confederate forces at the Battle of Bentonville.

place on North Carolina soil. On April 26, 1865, General Joseph E. Johnston surrendered the last Confedcrate troops to Union general William T. Sherman near Durham. The Civil War ended in 1865.

Sarah Malinda Pritchard Blalock of North Carolina disguised herself as a man by cutting her hair and wearing pants. She joined the Confederate Army to fight beside her husband during the Civil War.

As with many of the southern states, North Carolina was greatly affected by the war. Cities and farms lay in ruins. One result of the war was the freeing of slaves. But many slaves did not find their new lives easy. Some went to work for their former owners for extremely low wages. For the next three years the state struggled to rebuild its cities and government. In 1868 North Carolina rejoined the United States because it agreed to the federal government's plans for reconstruction. North Carolina was one of the first southern states to be readmitted to the Union

By 1880, North Carolina's farms had begun to recover. Huge amounts of tobacco as well as other crops were grown. In the Piedmont there was water, cheap land, and a steady supply of workers. Many of these workers were children. Cotton was grown nearby, and local cotton mills made cloth. Mill towns were set up around these businesses so the factory workers and their families could live together in one place.

Despite the number of new jobs being created, some people were not prospering. To help their families, many children were sent to work in the mills. The young workers often suffered under dangerous working conditions and long work hours. Times were also hard for North Carolina's African Americans. They faced discrimination because of their race.

This young girl works at the spinning machine of a cotton mill.

Most could not find well-paying jobs and were forced to live in poverty. People who lived in isolated areas or rural towns also struggled to get by.

Into the Twentieth Century

Despite these hardships, when the twentieth century began, North Carolinians still had good hopes for the future. On December 17, 1903, the Wright brothers took the world's first manned flight. For years the Wrights had been trying to build an airplane with an engine that would actually stay up in the air. Orville Wright's 12-second flight at Kill Devil Hill near Kitty

Hawk, on the coast of North Carolina, is now regarded as one of the greatest events in human history.

This was the first of many successes the state witnessed in the twentieth century. Over the next twenty-five years, North Carolina's tobacco and textile industries thrived. James B. Duke made a huge fortune from his American Tobacco Company. He used his money to establish Duke University in the 1920s. Today Duke is one of the nation's best universities, respected for both its academics and athletics.

Orville and Wilbur Wright built many planes and attempted several flights before succeeding in 1903.

The entire nation suffered in 1929 when the Great Depression started. Factories in North Carolina closed down. Many families moved to cities such as Durham, where a few tobacco factories and Duke University could still provide some jobs. Other families left the state and moved west in search of work. So many Americans lost their jobs during the Depression that President Franklin D. Roosevelt began one of several new programs. One program was the Works Progress Administration (WPA), which was designed to create jobs. As part of this program, the government hired hundreds of young men to start building the Blue Ridge Parkway.

North Carolina was greatly affected by World War II. Three military bases opened in the state. At the same time, factories that made much-needed war materials flourished. When

These African-American engineers were trained at Fort Bragg in 1942.

the men of North Carolina signed up to fight in the war, women took their places in the factories.

Many of the young men who had gone off to war took advantage of a new law that allowed veterans to go to college for free. This law was known as the GI Bill. After the war, many residents also benefited from the state's rapid industrial expansion. The cities of Raleigh, Durham, and Chapel Hill developed into important scientific centers. In the 1950s they became known as the Research Triangle. New industry brought people into North Carolina from many other states.

> Together with Pope Air Force Base, Fort Bragg in North Carolina, is one of the largest military complexes in the world.

Growing Pains

In the 1960s, the state played a key role in the growing civil rights movement. African Americans had long suffered from discrimination in North Carolina and elsewhere in the United States. Segregation laws prevented African Americans from doing many of the things that white citizens could do. They could not go to the same schools or sit next to white people in movie theaters or restaurants. North Carolina made newspaper headlines when a group of African Americans staged demonstrations protesting segregation. In 1960 African-American students from North Carolina A & T State University organized the first successful sit-in in American history. They entered a Woolworth's store in Greensboro, North Carolina, and seated themselves at its lunch counter to order lunch. When the manager told them they could not eat there, they refused to leave their seats. Through their courageous actions,

Four African-American college students protest segregation at the Woolworth's lunch counter in Greensboro.

> *Something had to happen.*
> *I watched how white people treated*
> *black people as if they were one step*
> *below human.*
>
> —Franklin McCain, a participant in the Greensboro sit-in

they helped to inspire others to join the civil rights movement. Eventually, Congress passed laws that ended discrimination based on the color of a person's skin.

Gradually, integration took place in the state's schools. A few communities resisted into the 1970s, but over time African Americans found more doors open to them. They began to win election to political offices on the local and state level.

By 1972, the state's newest concerns involved pollution. For years North Carolina's industries had been polluting the rivers. Citizens went to the polls and voted in favor of clean-water projects. It was the first of several steps residents took to ensure the future of their state.

Looking Forward

Throughout the end of the twentieth century, North Carolina's leaders have worked hard to bring about positive changes in the state. They have tried to encourage North Carolina to grow and prosper while also protecting its resources and natural beauty. Cities such as Durham started special programs to save their historic buildings while encouraging business leaders to build new factories and office buildings.

Today the state continues to make large and small changes all the time. North Carolinians sometimes express worry about what will happen next, but at the same time they work hard to make sure their future is bright.

Important Dates

1500 C.E. Native American groups live in what is now North Carolina.

1524 Explorer Giovanni da Verrazzano becomes the first European to see the coast of North Carolina.

1540 Explorer Hernando de Soto and his men search for gold and explore the southern part of present-day North Carolina.

1584 Sir Walter Raleigh sends several ships carrying settlers to the New World's first English colony on North Carolina's Roanoke Island.

Sir Walter Raleigh

1655 Nathaniel Batts becomes the first European to settle successfully in North Carolina, living there for many years.

1705 Bath, the first town in North Carolina, is built.

1776 On February 27, colonists fight British soldiers in North Carolina for the first time.

1789 North Carolina becomes the twelfth state.

1794 The capital of North Carolina is moved to the new city of Raleigh.

1840 The first public schools open in North Carolina.

1861 On May 20, North Carolina leaves the Union to join the Confederate States of America.

1865 From March 19 to 21, the Confederates in Bentonville lose the bloodiest Civil War battle fought in North Carolina.

1868 The state of North Carolina is readmitted to the United States.

1878 A Cherokee reservation is created in western North Carolina.

1903 The Wright brothers successfully fly an airplane with an engine.

1917 Three military bases open in North Carolina.

1937 North Carolina becomes the first state to establish soil and water conservation districts.

1954 Hurricane Hazel batters the North Carolina coast. It is the most destructive storm in the state's history.

Orville and Wilbur Wright

1960 A sit-in protesting segregation begins at a restaurant in Greensboro.

1984 In the NBA draft, UNC basketball star Michael Jordan is picked by the Chicago Bulls.

1996 Governor Jim Hunt is re-elected to a record fourth term.

2000 Beverly Purdue becomes North Carolina's first female lieutenant governor.

3 The People

Since the nation's earliest days, every ten years the U.S. government has taken a census, making an official count of the population. The last census took place in 2000. When the Census Bureau announced its results, North Carolinians found out their state had reached two new milestones. First, its population had topped 8 million. From 6.5 million in 1990, its population had risen to 8,049,313. Second, its jump in population made it the tenth-largest state. The census showed how quickly the state is growing. For the most part, North Carolinians are happy about the change. The state's tourist office likes to boast that North Carolina is "a better place to be." The fact that so many people continue to move there seems to prove that they are right.

North Carolina has always been home to a mix of people. According to the 2000 census, 72 percent of the state's population is white. Twenty-one percent is African American. Hispanics used to make up only a very small fraction of the population.

North Carolina's schools are filled with students who come from many different cultures.

Between 1990 and 2000, however, their numbers increased from 1 percent to 5 percent of the population. Less than 2 percent of North Carolinians are Asian or Asian American. Today the state's largest group of immigrants comes from Mexico. People from other countries and other parts of the United States also make North Carolina their home. They come to enjoy the climate and the many good things North Carolina has to offer.

In 1993, Sadie and Bessie Delany, two African-American sisters raised in Raleigh, made a sensation when, at the ages of 101 and 103, they published a memoir called *Having Our Say*. Their story was made into a hit Broadway play and a movie.

North Carolina's First Residents

Once Native Americans were the only people who inhabited North Carolina. However, as of the 2000 census, only 1.2 percent of the state's population is Native American. Despite this small percentage, North Carolina has the largest Native American population east of the Mississippi River. Most of the Native Americans in the state are Lumbee or Cherokee, but North Carolina is home to several different reservations. A few of the Native American groups in the state include the Eastern Band of Cherokee, the Lumbee, the Coharie, the Haliwa-Saponi, the Meherrin, the Indians of Person County, and the Southern Band Tuscarora.

These two Native Americans weave baskets in a Cherokee village.

Some Native Americans live on reservations while others live in towns and cities across the state. But Native American culture thrives throughout North Carolina. In the western part of the state, you will find the Oconaluftee Indian Village. This village shows what life was like in a Cherokee village in 1750. Guides teach visitors about Cherokee life and culture. The village has demonstrations of traditional activities such as building canoes, preparing food, and making pottery. This is just one of the many ways Native Americans in the state share their history and culture with others. Through museums, cultural centers, festivals, and powwows, North Carolina's Native Americans keep their culture and traditions alive.

Young Native Americans prepare for a tribal festival held in Asheville.

The People

Diversity

For centuries, people have traveled to North Carolina in search of prosperous lives. In the region's early days, the first settlers came from Europe. When North Carolina first became a colony, almost all of its settlers came from England or Scotland. There were just a few from France and Switzerland. In the seventeenth century, Africans were first brought by ship to North Carolina. There they were sold at market as slaves. Some African-American families in North Carolina are descended from these slaves. Other African Americans in the state come from other states or from other countries.

Over the next hundred years, immigrants started to arrive in North Carolina from Ireland and Germany. In 1752, several hundred Moravians from what is now the Czech Republic arrived. They came to North Carolina in search of religious freedom. After the Revolutionary War, immigrants arrived from a wider variety of European countries including Spain, Norway, Sweden, the Netherlands, and Italy.

All of these different ethnic groups made their own mark on North Carolina. They brought with them their own foods and special traditions, including music, dance, and celebrations. Over time, the people who settled in the mountains in the western part of the state developed their own culture. Living as they did in a very remote area, far from large towns or cities, they started a tradition of storytelling. They also came up with their own styles of music and dancing and became skilled in crafts such as whittling.

On the opposite end of the state, the people who settled on the Outer Banks also remained extremely isolated. As a result of living apart, some Outer Bankers, as they are called,

Traditional activities such as square dancing are still very popular around the state.

retained an old, distinctive dialect, or manner of speaking. North Carolinian Sheila Turnage states that one trait of this Outer Banks speech comes from the speakers keeping their lips close together when they speak. They make "i" sound like "oi," so they might say "the toid's hoigh" when they mean "the tide's high." The Outer Banks dialect also uses words not commonly heard in the rest of the country. During the past few decades, however, the Outer Banks has become less isolated. As a result, fewer Outer Bankers still use this unique dialect.

Famous North Carolinians

Billy Graham: Evangelist

North Carolina native Billy Graham was born and raised outside Charlotte. Graham is an evangelist, which means that he teaches and spreads Christianity to others. In the 1940s, he began to host a radio program and hold rallies. During the next fifty years he traveled all over the United States and around the world. Today he still appears on television once or twice a year and writes a daily newspaper column.

Michael Jordan: Athlete

Michael Jordan was born in New York, but he was raised and educated in Wilmington. Jordan became a basketball star while attending the University of North Carolina (UNC). He later joined the Chicago Bulls and led them to many victories. Jordan was so proud of UNC that he wore his UNC uniform shorts beneath his Bulls uniform in every game.

Dolley Madison: First Lady

Dolley Madison was born in North Carolina in 1768. She and her husband, James Madison, moved to Washington in 1801, when President Thomas Jefferson chose her husband to be his secretary of state. By this time, Jefferson's wife had died, so he often asked Dolley Madison to help him entertain at the White House. In 1809, James Madison was elected president, and Dolley Madison officially stepped into the role of First Lady.

Earl Scruggs: Musician

Earl Scruggs was born in the mountains of North Carolina in 1924. As a young man, Scruggs joined a band that toured all over the country. He and Lester Flatt later started their own band, called the Foggy Mountain Boys. They had many big hits in the 1960s, but from 1969 on Scruggs recorded mostly with his sons. In 1985, he was inducted into the Country Music Hall of Fame. Scruggs is considered to be one of the greatest bluegrass musicians and banjo players of all time.

Sequoyah: Native American Leader

Sequoyah was a Cherokee Indian born some time in the 1770s in a section of western North Carolina that is now a part of Tennessee. He was worried that the Cherokee who frequently spoke in English might forget how to speak their native language. In 1809 he developed a system for writing the Cherokee language. He spent twelve years completing this project. He also spent his time working for causes that would help the Cherokee. Sequoyah became so respected for his accomplishments that the giant redwood tree that grows in northern California was named for him.

O. Henry: Writer

William Sydney Porter was born in 1862 near Greensboro. He spent much of his youth in North Carolina, but also lived in places such as Texas, Honduras, and New York. Using the pen name O. Henry, Porter wrote hundreds of short stories. His stories were very popular because they were about common people and many could relate to them. Porter died in 1910. To honor Porter's achievements, every year the best American short stories are given the O. Henry Memorial awards.

Country Life and City Life

In the past, one thing most North Carolinians had in common was that they lived in the country or in very small towns. Recently, however, that has changed. Today, barely half of the population is rural. Both the eastern and the western sections of the state have smaller populations than the middle. The few towns in the Outer Banks, such as Nags Head, have small populations after their many visitors depart at the end of the summer. Along the shore, most towns have no more than a few thousand residents. Many of these places are old, with historic houses and two-lane roads that wind through fields, swamps, and pine tree groves. In the mountains to the west, there are mostly small towns. Some, such as Mortimer, are virtually ghost towns, places that were abandoned when a railroad or a factory closed down. Other towns, such as Boone, are thriving and face problems associated with too much growth.

In the mountains in the days before telephones, neighbors who lived far apart used a "distress holler" in times of emergency. This holler was a long, high call similar to a yodel. According to Leonard Emanuel, who was named National Hollerin' Champion in 1971, hollers helped when children were lost, men were drowning, and houses were on fire.

Though about half of the state's residents still live in small towns and rural areas, North Carolina's cities are growing at a faster rate than ever. Charlotte is officially the largest, with a population of roughly 540,000. A busy place, with a downtown full of skyscrapers, Charlotte is headquarters for many of the nation's banks, as well as companies that deal in insurance. Most people who work in the city do not choose to live there, but in one of the many suburbs that surround Charlotte. Even if they do not work there, many of them drive into the big city from time

Office buildings tower above this colorful sculpture in downtown Charlotte.

to time to attend sporting events or visit the city's other attractions.

Three of North Carolina's other major cities, Raleigh, Chapel Hill, and Durham, are each much smaller than Charlotte. Still, they are located close enough to form a large, overlapping area of suburbs, neighborhoods, and urban centers. Between Raleigh and Durham is an area called Research Triangle Park. This was especially planned as a place for high-tech companies to locate. Raleigh, as the state capital, has many government buildings and beautiful museums. Durham is home to Duke University and many medical research groups. One campus of the University of North Carolina is located in Chapel Hill, which is a city of gardens and quiet neighborhoods filled with old houses. The state's other large cities include Asheville, Greensboro, Winston-Salem, and Fayetteville.

Regardless of where they live, many North Carolinians share the same concerns. Poverty affects people living in the countryside, in the mountains, and in the cities. Especially in areas where jobs are hard to find, individuals and families are struggling to provide for themselves. Government programs do help the unemployed and the needy, but sometimes this is not enough. State leaders and concerned citizens are working together to find ways to help create more jobs and provide some form of assistance. State residents also want their state to develop a system that would provide good health care for all North Carolinians. Across the state, education

The People

Many North Carolinians believe that a top priority is providing a good educational system for the state's students.

remains an important issue. Children make up almost one quarter of the state's population and most of them enroll in the state's public schools. Parents, educators, and government leaders are working to improve the state's school system. Changes in all of these areas will take time and a lot of effort, but North Carolinians are committed to improving their state.

Fun in North Carolina

Not only does North Carolina have a large population of young people, it also has an unusually large number of senior citizens. This is because North Carolina is a popular place to retire. Almost one-eighth of the state's population is older than 65. Retired people move there for the state's outstanding scenery, its mild climate, and because there are many fun things to do there.

Fishers of all ages try their luck along the surf in Cape Hatteras.

Of course the population of North Carolina has a wide range of interests, but there are some things they especially enjoy. Lots of North Carolinians head outdoors when they have free time. Many avid hunters live in the state, as well as people who love to fish in the state's rivers, lakes, or in the ocean. In the winter, skiers head to the slopes. Hikers, campers, and bird-watchers especially enjoy North Carolina's state parks. The state has national parks, two national seashores, and many national forests.

North Carolinians are also big sports fans. Stock car racing is very popular. There are NASCAR raceways in Charlotte and

Fans at the Lowes Motor Speedway in Charlotte cheer for their favorite NASCAR drivers.

Rockingham. Many race car drivers live and practice in North Carolina. Famed driver Richard Petty's family comes from the Greensboro area. Basketball is also popular in North Carolina. The state has men's and women's professional teams, but also world-class university basketball teams. Duke and UNC are well known for their rivalry. The Durham Bulls is a minor-league baseball team so colorful that it inspired a movie called *Bull Durham*.

North Carolina's professional basketball teams are the Charlotte Bobcats (NBA) and the Charlotte Sting (WNBA). The Carolina Panthers are the state's NFL team and the Carolina Hurricanes represent the state in the NHL.

If there is one thing many North Carolinians love as much as sports, it is their state's history. Across the state genealogy and local history groups sponsor a range of events and activities. Preservation groups have raised money to preserve many of the state's historic sites and buildings. In addition, reenactors dress up in blue and gray uniforms, arm themselves

Women dressed in colonial clothing cook in the kitchen of Tryon Palace in New Bern. The palace became the state capitol after the Revolutionary War. Today it is a historical landmark and musuem.

with replica rifles and pistols, and stage the Civil War's Battle of Bentonville every March.

North Carolinians also support the arts. Especially in the larger cities and on the many college and university campuses, there are art shows, symphony concerts, and plays to attend. The state's long and proud musical heritage is also a big draw. Across the state there are performances of bluegrass, folk, country, rock, jazz, and traditional music.

"One North Carolina"

North Carolina is home to all sorts of people. Yet, whatever they do, however they choose to live, the people of North Carolina stand united in their great pride for their state. They like to brag about the many things that make the state special. Residents value the ways in which they differ but believe that deep down, "We are one North Carolina."

Calendar of Events

Azalea Festival
Every spring, thousands of visitors go to Wilmington to see the city's gardens. The gardens are filled with colorful azalea flowers in bloom. Visitors can also watch a parade and enjoy a street fair, art shows, and a tour of local homes.

Grifton Shad Festival
Each April the tiny town of Grifton hosts a celebration honoring the shad, a small fish that lives in the local creek. People come to hear live music, watch cloggers and other dancers, and listen to the outrageous fibs told in the lying competition.

The Coca-Cola 600 Auto Race
This is a favorite race for NASCAR fans. They come by the thousands to Lowe's Motor Speedway in Charlotte to watch stock cars speed around the track at 190 miles per hour.

National Hollerin' Contest
In the days before the telephone, mountain people hollered to their neighbors when they had a message to pass along. Every June, the town of Spivey's Corner is filled with people who have come to try to win the annual National Hollerin' Contest.

The Highland Games and Gathering of Scottish Clans
North Carolinians come to Grandfather Mountain to celebrate their state's Scottish heritage every July. They enjoy bagpipe music, dancing, food, costumes, and sports, such as wrestling and the caber toss. In this event, athletes throw a huge log that is about 20 feet long and weighs about 120 pounds.

Bagpipers at the Highland Games

The Craft Fair of the Southern Highlands

Members of the Southern Highland Craft Guild demonstrate their crafts and sell their work at this fair. This event takes place in Asheville twice a year, in July and October.

The Mountain Dance and Folk Festival

Mountain musicians and dancers come to Asheville every summer for this lively festival.

Mule Days

Many North Carolinians never miss Mule Days, held in Benson every September. There they can see a parade of hundreds of mules as well as mule races and a rodeo.

Cherokee Indian Fair

People come to learn all about the Cherokee at the Cherokee Indian Fair. This event is sponsored by the tribe every October in the town of Cherokee.

State Fair

North Carolina's State Fair is held every October in Raleigh. In addition to the rides and entertainment, the state's residents show off their livestock and enter pies, jams, and jellies in contests.

The Wright Brothers Anniversary Celebration

Every December Kitty Hawk holds a ceremony and celebration. This marks the day the Wright brothers completed the first manned airplane flight.

Fun at the state fair

4 How It Works

North Carolinians are served by their government at many different levels. City and county governments pass laws that affect people locally. The state government works for all of the residents of North Carolina. Finally, the state is also represented in the federal government. Citizens have the right to vote for the president every four years, and they also elect the officials who will represent the state in the U.S. Congress. Senators and representatives consider the best interests of state residents when they vote for or against legislation. Some laws that they pass affect every American. But North Carolina's representatives also introduce legislation that affects their state specifically.

State Government

Raleigh, as North Carolina's capital, is home to the state government. The governor's family lives in the executive mansion. The governor and lieutenant governor work in offices near the original state capitol. They work with the various departments

A statue of General Nathanael Greene stands near the Guilford battlegrounds in Greensboro. Greene was a general in the Colonial Army during the Revolutionary War.

and offices headed by the members of the Council of State and the cabinet. These departments—which include, for example, the department of transportation—are housed in office buildings also near the capitol. Many have branch offices in other parts of the state.

The general assembly, which starts a new session every year, has its own legislative building. When the general assembly is meeting, Raleigh is a busy place. That is because officials, citizens, and lobbyists—people who represent the interests of a certain industry—come to see the representatives and attend the legislative sessions.

Branches of Government

Executive The executive branch of North Carolina's state government includes the governor and lieutenant governor. The governor signs bills into law after the state's legislature passes them. Also included in the executive branch are members of the Council of State and the governor's cabinet. Members of the Council of State and the cabinet each head an agency, such as the Department of Corrections or the Agriculture Commission. Some of these department heads are elected, but others are appointed by the governor.

Legislative The state legislature is called the General Assembly and has two parts, the house of representatives and the senate. There are 50 state senators and 120 state representatives. The General Assembly makes the state's laws.

Judicial In North Carolina's judicial system, there are district and superior courts (where trials take place). The court of appeals and the supreme court look at cases in which groups or single citizens are unhappy with the decision made in an earlier case.

North Carolina's district and superior courts are scattered across the state. The supreme court, on the other hand, is located in a stately building in Raleigh. Lawyers go there to present their cases to the justices. The lawyers argue whether or not certain laws agree with the ideas set down in the state's constitution.

Local Governments

Decisions that affect the residents of a town are made by their local government. Each of North Carolina's hundreds of towns and cities has its own mayor and town or city council. They make laws regarding issues such as deciding what types of buildings and businesses can be built near people's homes. They also

This statue of Presidents James K. Polk, Andrew Jackson, and Andrew Johnson stands outside of the state Capitol. President Jackson is on horseback, President Polk is shown holding a map, while President Johnson holds the U.S. Constitution.

appoint a police force. The state has one hundred counties, each with its own government. North Carolina law says that every county must have its own elected board of commissioners. The county commissioners choose a county manager. In other states, county governments take care of roads. But that is one task that they do not perform in North Carolina. Instead, the commissioners' main jobs are to oversee a board of education, a board of health, and a board of social services.

Three American presidents were born in North Carolina: James K. Polk, Andrew Jackson, and Andrew Johnson.

How North Carolina's Laws Are Made

North Carolina's state laws start out as bills. Sometimes a citizen has an idea for a new law and contacts his or his representative to suggest it. Other times, state representatives, senators, or members of their staffs come up with the idea. The governor or another state official may also suggest an idea to a member of the general assembly.

To start the lawmaking process, a member of the state's general assembly introduces the bill into the state house of representatives or senate. After the bill's title is read out loud, it is assigned a number and sent to a special committee that looks closely into every aspect of the bill. The committee discusses the positive and negative aspects of the bill. If it needs to, the committee does research. Then it votes on the bill. The bill is then discussed by the entire state senate or house of representatives, depending upon where it was first introduced. Sometimes it is then amended, or changed.

If the members vote in favor of the bill, it is sent to the other branch of the General Assembly, which follows the same process. If its members vote in favor of a bill but make changes to it, they must send it back to the first branch for another vote. Most bills that are finally approved by both houses in the General Assembly then go to the governor. He or she has the right to veto, or reject, a bill. When this happens, the bill goes back to the General Assembly for yet another vote. If the bill

The state legislature used to meet at the State Capitol, which was completed in 1840. Today, the legislature meets in a different building in Raleigh.

then receives votes from more than three-fifths of the representatives, it becomes a law. Bills that the governor does not veto automatically become laws.

Getting Involved

Throughout the state's history, North Carolinians have taken an active part in their government. Concerned citizens called attention to issues associated with such things as the environment, the budget, education, and crime. A lot of the state's legislation is shaped by the voice of the people. By learning about state issues and local concerns you can make a difference too.

To contact North Carolina's state legislators go to this Web site:
http://www.ncga.state.nc.us/GIS/Representation/Who_Represents_Me/Who_Represents_Me.html

Making a Living

From the Land

When the first European explorers arrived in North Carolina, the Native Americans who lived in the region were farmers, hunters, and fishers. In order to make fields for crops, some Native Americans cut down and burned trees in parts of the forests. The first settlers from Europe copied these methods when they started their own farms. After a few years of farming the land, however, some of the soil grew weak and could no longer produce healthy plants. When this happened settlers moved to new lands in the region to begin again. Eventually farmers found that tobacco could easily grow in fertile areas. It became the region's main crop. Many farms also grew cotton that was used to make fabric.

Today, however, agriculture makes up only about 2 percent of the state's total income. There are around 56,000 farms in the state. Many farmers raise livestock such as hogs, cattle, and poultry. They also plant various crops including, tobacco, corn, soybeans, peanuts, and sweet potatoes.

Tourism is an important part of North Carolina's economy.

Recipe for Sweet Potato Pie

Sweet potatoes are an important North Carolina crop. This recipe shows you how to use them in a simple but tasty dessert.

Ingredients:

9 inch unbaked pie crust
2 1/2 cups cooked and mashed sweet
   potatoes
1 cup evaporated milk
2 large eggs
1 1/4 cup white sugar
1/2 cup butter
1/2 teaspoon cinnamon
1 1/2 teaspoon vanilla extract

Combine all the ingredients in a large bowl. Beat the mixture until it is well blended. You can use an electric mixer to make your job a little easier. Pour the mixture into the pie crust.

Have an adult help you with the oven. Bake the pie at 425 degrees Fahrenheit for ten minutes. Then reduce the heat to 350 degrees and bake for approximately 55 minutes. Insert a knife into the center of the pie. If it comes out clean the pie is done, otherwise, cook for a few more minutes.

Allow the pie to cool after baking. When it is cool, serve it with some nuts or whipped cream and enjoy!

Lumber

Logging became important in North Carolina when George Washington and five other men started a lumber company. They planned to drain water from 40,000 acres of land in the Great Dismal Swamp in the northeastern corner of the state. Once the swamp was dry they wanted to cut down the trees, sell the wood, and use the cleared land for farms. However, draining the swampy land was more difficult than they expected and soon they focused mainly on harvesting the lumber. Many cypress trees growing in the swamp were cut down and used for shipbuilding. Cedar trees were used for shingles and other wood products. Lumber from other parts of the state was used to make furniture.

A truck filled with lumber heads down from the mountains.

With so many dense forests, logging is still an important industry in the state. Only Georgia, Alabama, and Oregon have more forestland than North Carolina. Most of the trees cut down are used to make paper or furniture. The town of Hickory is the center of the state's furniture industry, with more than half of its furniture factories located there. The town is an important center for furniture sales. North Carolina is also one of the largest producers of Christmas trees.

Mining

In the early nineteenth century, North Carolina became a center for gold mining. In 1799, gold was found on a farm in Cabarrus County. This turned out to be an area rich in mineral deposits. In 1823, a survey of the Gold Hill area showed that there were other formations in the region that might contain gold. In the years that followed many people searched for gold in the area. They only found small pieces until 1842, when the first vertical mine shaft was dug. It allowed miners to find large amounts of gold. Today there is a historic park at what is called the Barnhardt shaft, named after the man who paid for the digging. One year later, another prospector, Peter Earnhardt, found gold in the Randolph shaft, which was located across the road from the Barnhardt shaft. The Randolph claim produced a huge supply of gold. It was the richest and deepest gold mine on the North American continent east of the Mississippi River. It is estimated that the gold shipped out of the Gold Hill area was worth $6 million. One-third of that was from the Randolph shaft. The growth of mining in North Carolina prompted the U.S. government to build a mint in Charlotte. Today that mint is a museum.

Gold mining is no longer very common in the state. But other products are mined from the land. During the eighteenth century, North Carolinians made and sold bricks made from the red clay found in the Piedmont. At that time fireplaces and woodstoves were often used. Clay tiles were needed for the chimneys and roofs because the clay would not catch on fire. For a time this was a profitable industry. Today, North Carolinians mine clay, sand and gravel, and crushed stone. Much of the sand, gravel, and stone is used in construction. As of the year 2000, North Carolina was second in gemstone mining.

The state provides a large amount of the world's lithium. This is a soft metal that is used in items such as batteries and nuclear weapons.

Granite from North Carolina's quarries is used in construction in the state and in other parts of the country.

Products & Resources

Tobacco

Even though North Carolina grows less tobacco each year, this green leaf remains the state's number one crop. North Carolina grows more tobacco than any other state.

Turkeys

Poultry is big business in the state. Farmers raise 47 million turkeys a year. This makes North Carolina the nation's largest producer of the meat that appears on so many tables every Thanksgiving.

Minerals

North Carolina mines produce large quantities of feldspar, crude mica, and olivine, which are sold around the world. Feldspar is used in making glass and ceramics.

Pine

North Carolina's lumber industry uses pine and other types of trees to make lumber, furniture, and paper.

Computers and Electronic Products

North Carolina exports billions of dollars worth of goods to foreign countries. It exports more computers and electronic products than anything else.

Sweet Potatoes

The sweet potato is North Carolina's official vegetable. It is also a profitable industry. According to the North Carolina Sweet Potato Commission, the state produces around 40 percent of the nation's sweet potatoes.

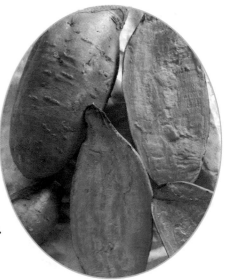

Manufacturing

Presently the state makes most of its money—31 percent—through manufacturing, or making goods. There are many high-tech industries in the Research Triangle, where Raleigh, Durham, and Chapel Hill meet. Workers there research new technologies and manufacture the most up-to-date electronic products. These include fiber optics, computer hardware and software, lasers, and robots. The state still earns money by manufacturing products out of harvested lumber.

Men and women who work on microelectronic parts wear protective clothing so that the tiny components remain clean and undamaged.

Tourism, Sales, and Service

Tourists spend billions of dollars in North Carolina every year. Many come to see the state's natural and historic wonders. Throughout the year, vacationers travel to North Carolina to enjoy the outdoors and the mild climate. Sporting events also attract many visitors.

Selling products is another major source of the state's income. North Carolinians also earn their livings through finance, insurance, and real estate. Some of the world's biggest banks have headquarters in North Carolina.

Over the years, the economy of North Carolina can be expected to change even more. North Carolinians will need to work hard to make sure the changes will be good and that their state will continue to prosper. With their ability to work together and to adapt to the times, the people of the Tar Heel State look with confidence to a bright future.

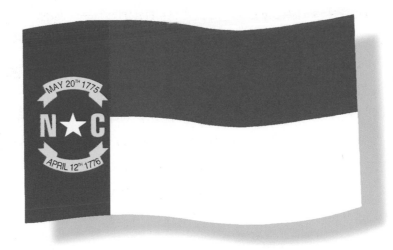

The right-hand side of the flag has a horizontal red stripe with a white stripe below it. The left-hand side of North Carolina's flag has a vertical blue stripe. In the center of the stripe are the letters N and C. The words May 20th 1775, are written above the two letters. This is said to be the date when Mecklenburg County declared independence from Great Britain. The words April 12th 1776 run below the N and C. This was the day when North Carolinians declared independence from any foreign nation.

The state seal shows two women. One woman stands, holding a scroll with the word Constitution on it. She represents liberty. The other woman is seated with crops. She represents plenty. Behind the women are mountains and a ship on the ocean. The state motto appears along the bottom of the seal. It means "to be rather than seem." The dates on the state flag are also found on the seal.

State Flag and Seal

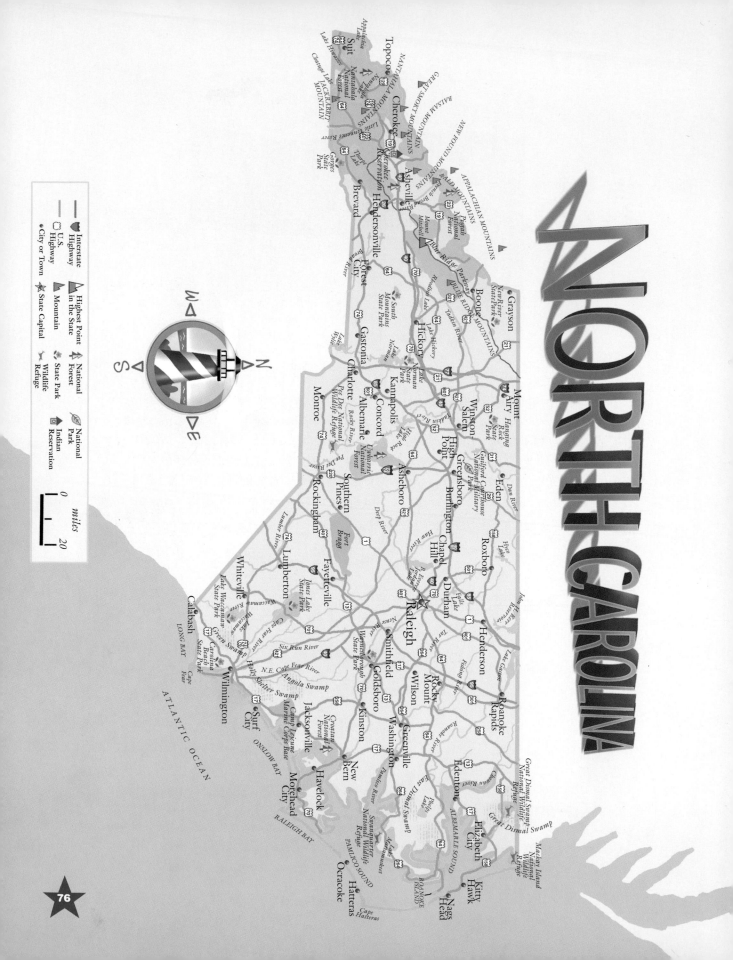

NORTH CAROLINA

Legend:

- Interstate Highway
- U.S. Highway
- City or Town
- Highest Point in the State
- Mountain
- State Park
- State Capital
- National Forest
- National Park
- Indian Reservation
- Wildlife Refuge

miles 0 20

ATLANTIC OCEAN

Suit
Topoco
Cherokee
Cherokee Reservation
Brevard
Hendersonville
Forest City
Asheville
Grayson
Gastonia
Charlotte
Monroe
Rockingham
Southern Pines
Whiteville
Lumberton
Fayetteville
Calabash
Wilmington
Surf City
Jacksonville
Morehead City
Havelock
Ocracoke
Hatteras
Nags Head
Kitty Hawk
Elizabeth City
Edenton
New Bern
Washington
Greenville
Kinston
Goldsboro
Wilson
Rocky Mount
Henderson
Roanoke Rapids
Durham
Raleigh
Smithfield
Chapel Hill
Burlington
Roxboro
Asheboro
Greensboro
High Point
Eden
Winston-Salem
Concord
Albemarle
Kannapolis
Hickory
Boone
Mount Airy

The Old North State

Words by William Joseph Gaston

Car - o - li - na! Car - o - li - na! heav-en's bless-ings at - tend her, While we live we will ___ cher - ish, pro - tect and de - fend her, Tho' the scorn - er may ___ sneer at and wit - lings de - fame her. Still our hearts swell with ___ glad - ness when - ev - er we name her. Hur - rah! Hur - rah! the Old North State for - ev - er, Hur - rah! Hur - rah! the good Old North Srate.

State Song

More About North Carolina

Books

Ellis, Marion A. and Howard E. Covington, Jr. *North Carolina Century: Tar Heels Who Made a Difference, 1900–2000*. Charlotte, NC: Museum of the New South, 2002.

Hicks, Ray. *The Jack Tales*. New York: Callaway, 2000.

Powell, William S. *North Carolina: A History*. Chapel Hill: University of North Carolina Press, 1988.

Whedbee, Charles Harry. *Outer Banks Mysteries and Seaside Stories*. Winston-Salem, NC: John F. Blair, 1985.

Web Sites

North Carolina Museum of History:
http://ncmuseumofhistory.org

The Official Web site for the State of North Carolina:
http://www.ncgov.com

Tour the State Capitol:
http://www.ah.dcr.state.nc.us/sections/capitol/stat_cap/tour.htm

We Are One North Carolina Poetry and Artwork Contest Web page:
http://www.ncgov.com/asp/subpages/we_are_one_nc.asp

About the Author

Ann Graham Gaines is a freelance writer and picture researcher, whose first book for children was published in 1991. She and her family live near Gonzales, Texas. North Carolina is one of her favorite places to visit.

Index

Page numbers in **boldface** are illustrations.

Minna looked out her bedroom window at the nighttime sky. "Twinkle, twinkle, little star. How I wonder what you are . . ." She thought for a moment. "I wonder . . . what . . . stars . . . are?"

"When I was your age," said Mom, "I loved going stargazing with my dad and wondering about stars."

"What did you wonder?" asked Minna.

"I wondered, *Where do stars go during the day? How far away are stars?* I gave them names like Sparkly and Brighty."

"And Twinkly!" said Minna.

They giggled.

"The Children's Museum has a new place called Star Space," said Mom. "Would you like to invite a few friends to come for supper, visit Star Space, and then go stargazing?"

"Yay!" said Minna. "A star party!"

Friday afternoon, Minna and Dad made supper.

⭐ Star Supper Recipes ⭐
Ask an adult to help!

Star Soup

You will need:

⅓ cup uncooked star-shaped pasta
  (also called stelline)
¾ cup mixed frozen peas and carrots
2 14-oz. cans of chicken, vegetable, or beef broth

★ Bring the broth to a boil in a 2-quart saucepan.
★ Add the pasta, stir, and cook for 6 minutes over medium heat.
★ Add the peas and carrots and cook for 4 more minutes.
  Serves 6
  (You can also buy canned soup with pasta stars
  already in it and heat it according to the directions.)

Star Sandwiches

★ Cut bread into star shapes with a star cookie cutter and make your favorite sandwich.

Star cookies

★ Buy butter-cookie dough.
★ Cut out star shapes with the cookie cutter.
★ Bake according to directions.

Slices of **star fruit**
  (also called carambola)

star cookie cutter

star sandwich

star fruit

star cookie

6

Friday evening, Tyrone, Maya, Dave, and Lindsey came over.
They ate star-shaped sandwiches, star soup, star-shaped cookies,
and tasted star fruit.

Then Mom drove them to Star Space.

STAR SPACE

STAR SPACE
A NEW branch of
the Children's Museum

"Welcome to Star Space!" said their guide. "My name is Stellan, and I think that stars are WONDER–full. What do *you* wonder about stars?"

"I wonder what's the closest star?"

"I wonder how many stars there are."

"What shapes are stars?"

"I wonder about soccer stars, and is the Milky Way made out of stars . . . or candy bars?"

"I'm Minna. I wonder what stars are."

Stellan smiled. "You've asked a lot of stellar questions. So let's travel together through Star Space."

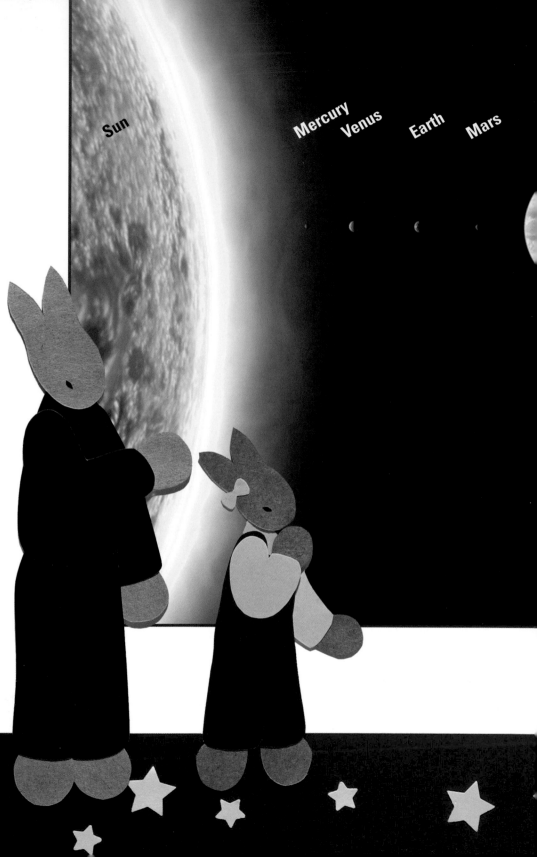

"Here's a picture of our solar system," said Stellan. "Does anyone know which star is closest to the Earth?"

Tyrone said, "Planets go around the sun. They aren't stars. Moons go around the planets. They aren't stars."

Minna asked, "Is it our sun? Is our sun a star?"

Sun   Mercury Venus   Earth   Mars

"Yes," said Stellan. "The sun is the only star in our solar system. Guess how long it takes the light from our sun star to reach Earth?"

"An hour?" asked Maya.

"Two days?" asked Dave.

"Good guesses," said Stellan, "but it takes . . . only . . . about . . . eight minutes!"

"Eight minutes!" said Minna. "It takes me longer to walk to school!"

Then Stellan asked, "Guess what day of the week is named for our star?"

Moon

Earth

92,960,000 miles from the sun

"SUNDAY!" they all shouted.

"Right!" said Stellan. "You are stars for getting that answer right."
Mom asked, "Where do stars go during the day, Stellan?"

Venus
57,241,000 miles from the sun

Mercury
35,985,000 miles from the sun

Sun
Our sun, our star.

Our sun was born about 4.6 billion years ago.
Temperature: 10,000° F on the surface
Sunlight travels at 186,282 miles per second.

Model made by Luna (not to scale)

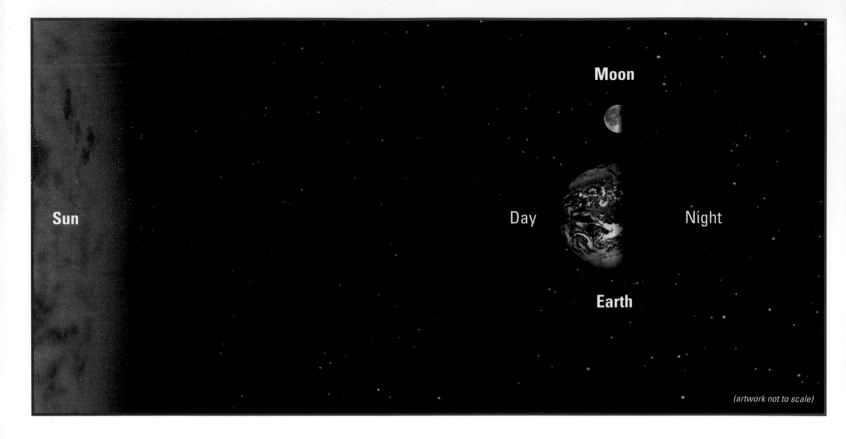

Moon

Sun

Day

Night

Earth

(artwork not to scale)

"Stars are in the sky night *and* day," said Stellan. "We just can't see them in the daytime because our sun's light is so bright."

Tyrone added, "My dad says, 'Don't ever, ever look right at our sun star. Even with sunglasses, you'll damage your eyes.' "

"That's very important advice," said Stellan.

Minna asked, "Stellan, are shooting stars *stars*?"

"Good question!" said Stellan. "They aren't. Shooting stars are tiny bits of dust and rock that burn up when they enter the Earth's atmosphere. . . . Minna, I think you also wondered, *What are stars*? Stars are suns!"

"Stars are suns," Minna whispered.

Stellan nodded. "They are fiery balls of burning gases. Stars give off enormous light and heat. They are thousands of degrees on the outside and millions of degrees on the inside."

"Cool! I mean *hot*!" said Tyrone. "I wonder if stars ever run out of gas."

"They do, but that takes billions and billions of years!" said Stellan. "At night, we may be looking at the light from a star that burned out long ago, but its light is still traveling from outer space. Let's travel on. . . ."

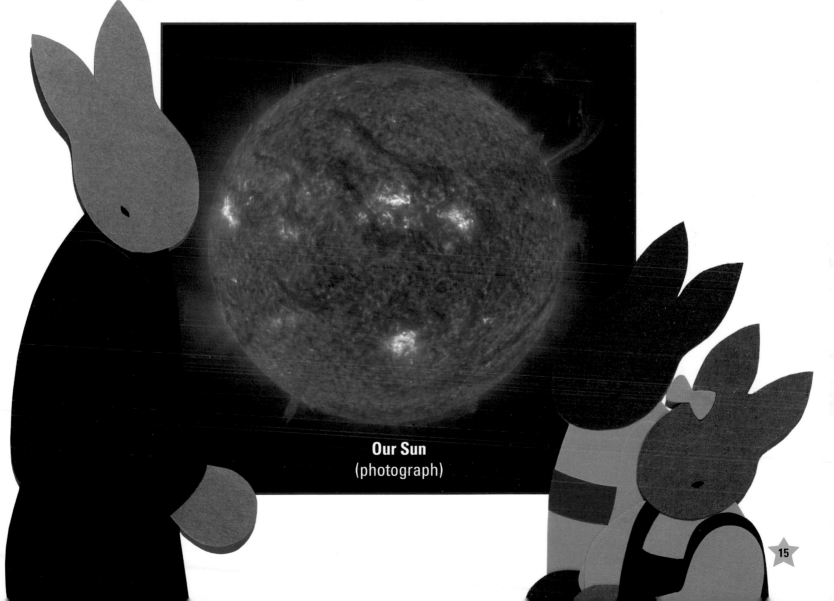

Our Sun
(photograph)

15

Next Stellan explained, "Astronomers are scientists who look at stars, wonder about stars, and study and learn about stars. The word *astronomer* is from the Greek words *astron*, which means star, and *nomer*, which means namer."

"Star . . . *namer*!" they shouted.

"Yes!" said Stellan. "I'm an amateur astronomer. I use a telescope to look at stars and to see them better, since they are trillions of miles away. You can use binoculars, too. Wouldn't it be exciting to go stargazing, discover a new star, and name it?"

"When I discover a new star, I'll call it Dave," said Dave.

"We're going stargazing later!" said Minna.

Why do stars twinkle?

Starlight bends and scatters as it travels through the Earth's atmosphere.

New **Moon phases** Full
29½ day cycle

Stargazing Forecast
Tonight: Excellent
New moon
Clear sky
Sunset: 6:48 p.m.

STARGAZING
NIGHT SKY
OUR SUN, OUR STAR
Outer Space
THE CONSTELLATIONS
GALAXIES
Ast...
Sylvie's Wishing Star

Welcome to the Star Garden.
Wonder and Learn and Grow!

17

Stellan handed them each a star card and lined them up. "Stars are different sizes, different brightnesses, and different colors. A star's color tells us its temperature. Blue stars are the hottest."

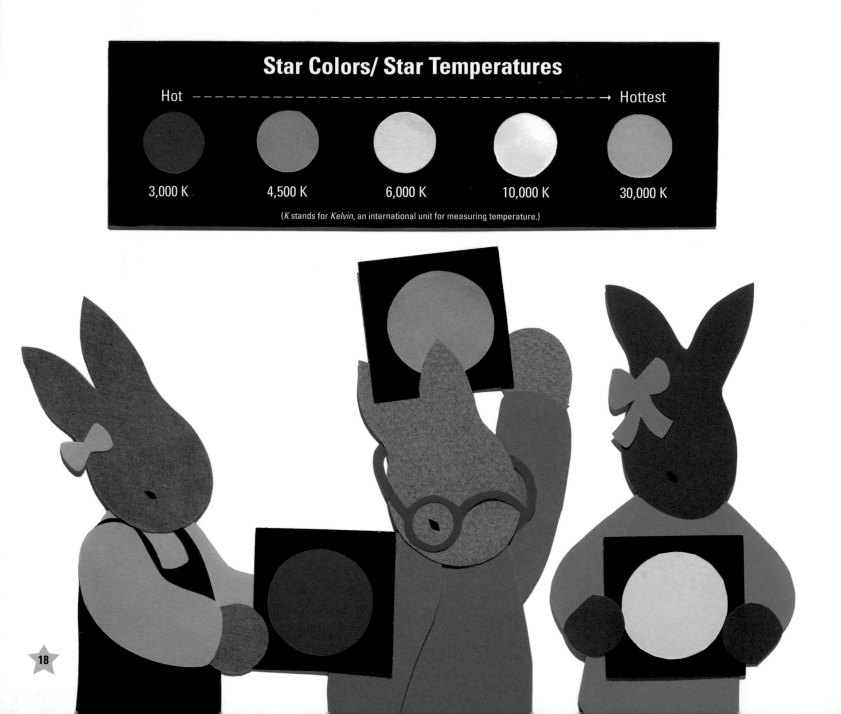

Star Colors/ Star Temperatures

Hot – → Hottest

| 3,000 K | 4,500 K | 6,000 K | 10,000 K | 30,000 K |

(*K* stands for *Kelvin*, an international unit for measuring temperature.)

"If I discovered a red star, I'd name it Ruby!" said Minna.
"I'd like to discover a white one. I'd call it Marshmallow," said Maya.

"Good names," said Stellan. "And imagine, there are about one hundred million, trillion stars in the universe."
"That's a lot of stars to name!" said Tyrone.
"It is. So now when new stars are discovered, they are given numbers as names. All the billions of stars we see at night are called . . .

follow me . . .

Our Galaxy

. . . the Milky Way," said Stellan. "The Milky Way is our galaxy."

"Wow!" said Lindsey.

"It looks swirly," said Minna.

"When you're ready," said Stellan, "we can go see photographs of other galaxies taken from outer space."

They looked a little longer.

The Milky Way

21

Hubble Space Telescope
(Model by Celeste)

Other Galaxies

Andromeda Galaxy

Whopper Galaxy

"There are many, many galaxies," said Stellan.

"Galaxies look like paintings in a museum," said Tyrone.

"Galaxies are beautiful!" said Minna.

"I think so too," said Stellan.

Cartwheel Galaxy

Bode's Galaxy

Sombrero Galaxy

Stars are *trillions* of miles away.

How big is a *trillion*?

100	one hundred
1,000	one thousand
1,000,000	one million
1,000,000,000	one billion
1,000,000,000,000	one trillion

The distance a star's light travels in a year is called a *light year*.

Their next stop was the Star Space Activity Stations. They got busy.

Starlight! Star bright!
First star I see tonight,
wish I may,
wish I might
have the wish
I wish tonight.

Star Station:
Make a wishing star
and then
make a wish.

24

Star Station:
Paint a creation.

25

"A boat?" said Minna.

They all climbed in.

"Long ago, sailors and travelers looked at the stars to help them find their way," said Stellan.

Star Station: Navigation

"Look up," said Stellan.

They looked up at a painting on the ceiling.

Stellan explained, "Constellations are groups of stars that look like patterns. The Big Dipper and the Little Dipper are in the shape of pots, or dippers, with handles. Count the stars in the Big Dipper."

They counted. "One, two, three, four, five, six, seven."

"Hey! The Little Dipper has seven stars too!" said Minna.

"The last star in the Little Dipper's handle is a very important star. It's called the North Star. It always looks as if it's in the same place in the sky," said Stellan.

"Is it kind of like a compass in the sky?" asked Tyrone.

"That's right," said Stellan. "Lots of stories have been made up about the patterns of stars in the nighttime sky. Let's go to the last Star Station – constellations."

The Little Dipper
Part of the constellation Ursa Minor/The Little Bear

The North Star
The Pole Star, also called Polaris

The Big Dipper
Part of the constellation Ursa Major/The Big Bear

Pointers
always point to the North Star.

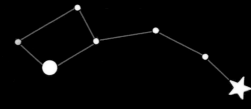

Artwork by Ray

Stellan continued, "Ancient Greeks thought that Orion was the biggest, strongest, best hunter. Look for Orion's belt – three bright stars in a line. The bright star in his left shoulder is called Betelgeuse."

They laughed. "Beetle juice!"

"Look for Cass-see-oh-pee-ah. Cassiopeia was a queen," said Stellan. "Part of her constellation is her chair. Sometimes it looks like a *W*. Sometimes it looks like an *M*."

"I see an *M*," said Maya.

"The constellation Canis Major has the brightest star," said Stellan. "It's called Sirius."

"I see it," said Dave. "Serious-ly."

Mom looked at her watch. "The sun has set. It's a clear night. Time to go stargazing!"

"Have fun," said Stellan. "Come back soon."

Star Station: Constellations— Look and Find

Northern Hemisphere/Spring Constellations

Stella is the Latin word for "star." There are eighty-eight named constellations.

Artwork by Robert

They threw on their jackets, ran outside, and climbed to the top of the hill — far away from the lights of town. It took a little time for their eyes to adjust to the darkness.

They spread out an old quilt
on top of the sheet of plastic
Mom had brought so they
wouldn't feel cold or get wet
from the dew.

Then they lay down,
gazed up at the stars, . . .

and they were filled with

wonder!

GO STARGAZING!

Make
a wishing star.
Make a wish.

Create
a picture of your star
using
art materials.

★ Go on a clear new-moon night, when the sky is darkest.

★ Go when the weather forecast is for clear skies.

★ Wear a warm jacket.

★ Bring a lounge chair and/or a blanket to sit on.

★ Bring a flashlight.

★ If you have a night sky constellation map or a planisphere, bring red cellophane and a rubber band to cover the light. That will make it easier to look at the stars after you study the chart.

★ Go where there is the least light pollution.

Be filled with wonder.

If you
discovered a star,
what would
you name it?

What do you
wonder about
the stars?

Write a story
about
your star.

Write
a short star poem.
It can rhyme
but it doesn't
have to.

Learn more
about stars:

Visit a Planetarium,
an Observatory,
a Space Center;

Read books about the stars;

Go to the
NASA website for kids.